POEMS AND PEONIES

POEMS AND PEONIES

CHELSIE DIANE

POEMS AND POWER

for clara, lilly, and jack

poems

spoiler alert.

you write twenty-two thousand more poems.

you fire your agent.

women keep coming to your class
they keep coming and coming and coming
and coming and coming.

your mother dies without saying she's proud of you.

the lover that paints you never calls
never. not once after you sleep with him
you check your phone for three years
and never. chelsie. never.
not once does he call.

the cancer never comes back
until you are very old
and very ready.

the kids never drown in the ocean
or get kidnapped from a target.
your jeep never rolls down the canyon.
a coyote never eats your cat.

your book gets published.
and that one too.
oh and that
my god that
that will be a surprise.

one of your daughters is gay
(thank god)

you go to greece
and france
and walk ten thousand more miles

letting every lesser love move through you
like air like air like air

you give a ted talk
and let me tell you
you give thousands of more teds
a tallllk.

you finally find a skincare routine
that doesn't break you out like a 14-year-old boy.

you run another marathon.

your ex-husband remarries this year
there is a barbecue for one of your children's
birthdays
he's holding his new baby
in his new backyard
with his new wife
he has to flip a steak
he hands you the baby.

you marry again.
a few people sit on old quilts
he never not once takes his eyes off you
you have antique rings you engrave
he's not scared of you
he's old enough to lose his mind over road head
he calls you star. he calls you finally.
you leave him poems on the breakfast table
he makes a mosaic peony out of glass you broke
you call him a pain in the ass.
you call him all day long.
you call him
your sun.
your entire fucking sun.
your king.
your sun god king.

there is one morning you never forget
not ever

not when you are 43 the day you move to europe
not when you are 54 and thinking about botox
not when you are 63 and holding your third grandchild
not when you are 98 letting go of their hand

you are standing across the living room
holding your old cross-eyed cat
after he made you tea
and you stop.
you stop.
and you say
this is my life.
this is my life.
this is my life.

in another life
i'm standing in a courtroom
between my lawyer that wrote emails in all caps
because of his eyesight but also
he was always yelling
and the man that took my virginity
that fell asleep in the plastic hospital chair
while i pushed out his ten-pound son.
the number isn't rent
and i don't ask for more
just the kids to get out of the car
and as they walk into his house
with the suitcases i had their names printed on the first christmas
i don't look. i sink my nails into the steering wheel
board a one-way ticket to trastevere and rent a room
with a sheer curtain over an alley window
in a year i am fluent and sit naked for emiliano
holding a snake
he paints my breasts as they are
lopsided sucked slopes from mouths
he'll never hear
i don't have health insurance or a car
i have a couple candles in wine bottles
two waitressing jobs
and more longing than a poet should
i call every few days
my daughters tell me about their stepmom
and all her kids and i make empty promises
until they stop asking
etch the years into the thousand-year-old wall
like the count of monte cristo in his cell
by my mattress where i let the painter with black eyes
and freckle on his lip fuck me but not hold me
because how. could. i. be. held.
after a year
i am at the roman market
buying hand-cut tagliatelle
i hear *mommy* and when i turn
she reaches for a mother that stayed

i buckle like a half-boiled noodle over the pot
the fire beneath
as if my middle and everything it grew
is cut from me again
i lose lumbar spine
and crumble in a life i chose
in another life i go to the louvre
and see the venus up close
the thousand hairline cracks in the paint
and i only wonder how she kept standing
i am human
and when lost with no sign of shore
i too think of other ways to be birthed
from a shell or from surrender
i know some see the next wave and know they'll
choose to let it fold their body under
and some pick a direction and fight until muscle stops
and when they wash up on different days
we think of only
how they moved the water
as best they could
both drowning in ways
we'd never think to judge.

beautiful creature
it's time to forgive yourself
you were surviving

when i am an old woman

a man will send me a poem and i will tell him *truthfully it's shit.*
i'll yell at the mansplainer on the public bus
she knows! she knows already
shut up! she knows!
i'll stay up all night helping
my daughter latch the baby to her breast
i'll spray my letters with a love spell
containing a drop of my own blood
i'll take each grandchild to the country of their choice
gift them a stray kitten to piss off their mothers
i'll be late to thanksgiving dinner
because i sailed to catalina island that morning
to eat what i caught
i will hand type on my 44 royal
a letter to all my children
that simply says
i love you. i am done apologizing now.
they will find my shrooms at tsa
i'll bite small dogs and small children back
i will tell the boutiques
fake plants should be punishable by death!
i will call up all of my old lovers
and say *hello! this is chelsie diane speaking*
and i called to tell you today you are entirely full of shit!

at 93 i'll fly to florence
knock on the italian painter's door
unbutton my dress slowly
and say *paint me*
as venus unshelled
as the raven
as the mother
as falling water
and the lover
as the standing again
as the war and
ancient fire

and the ache
paint me
as a woman
that was brave.

dolly parton knew exactly what she was doing when
she married carl.

carl minding his own business with a cigar.
carl leaning against a fencepost of their tennessee mountain home.
carl a man of few words never jealous a day in his life.
porter wagoner and kenny rogers ain't got shit on carl.
carl is steady. carl would never fuck around with jolene.
carl has a massive d. carl is probably a taurus.
carl drives a truck through toad hollar and never gets it stuck.
carl gets the flu once every five years
and fights it with jalapeños and moonshine.

listen up! lover that is 50 years old still healing his mother wound!
listen up! lover on a two-week silent retreat!
lover that waits until i'm sick to call me that
they've changed their mind!
the ocean is too cold in california!

listen up lover boys.
i have decided i have the energy of dolly fucking parton
and therefore i will have her partner!

you must feel like honeysuckle and junebugs and church bells and
casseroles and a porch swing to have a second of my time.
or wait in line! i have autographs to sign.

when i'm on tour carl isn't calling me saying
he got so high he saw jesus!
carl is chasing the paparazzi off our lawn with a rifle!

carl is not in rehab or feeling insecure that i'm on the radio again.
carl is pulling carrots out of the garden with his leathered hands.

carl says nothing about the fuscia butterfly rug or my 227th wig.
carl is handwriting a check to the electric company.

carl isn't doing ayahuasca with naked women in joshua tree
carl is winterizing the rv.

carl isn't having lunch with his ex
or starting a men's makeup line
or clubbing in miami
carl is reading the farmers' almanac
and frying an egg for the dog.

listen. dolly is tired.
she's been weeks on the road
and has a whole world to sing to.

and when i get home in the middle of the night
i want carl waiting up at the table.
i want carl waiting at my table
to unbutton rhinestones.
to say
welcome home!
welcome home dolly!

the next man that tells you
you came from his rib
remind him it takes you 9 months
to make that rib
along with every other bone
inside his body

listen this world will kill us all.
every one of us.
but first

someone somewhere has discovered they
stop stuttering when they read poetry

the loneliest panda on earth has given birth

someone caught in a downpour
on some city street
has surrendered and laughing
lifts their palms

a five cm cuddlefish has attached her hundred eggs
to the underside of a shell

a whale has made her 3000 mile migration home
singing the whole way!

a mama cow has jumped a fence to get to her baby

a dehydrated flamingo sits on her egg for twenty-eight days
and feeds her chick salt and her own blood

someone sees a book in the window
written by an old lover
will soon find that every word
was written about them

someone has quit their horrible
corporate job and made a scene!

a child wakes from surgery with a heart
that their body loves

a bride has just looked up to see her true love
at the back of the church

in a small town locker room
a coach tells nine boys he loves them

a couple too young and too in love
is pawning all for a one-way ticket

a child has put on a cape and is on the ledge!

somewhere someone has had their last first date
and left the candles burning all night

a dying mother tells her daughter
the curtains are angels
coming for her

someone has broken no contact
drove all night
and is knocking

and somewhere i swear to god
is a poet
that doesn't yet know it
hurting unimaginably
scribbling a line
on a napkin
that will live in you.

my children are in the ocean
and last week a drone over escondido beach
captured eighteen great whites weaving in and out of hundreds of
human bodies in lycra
one of the shadows is nine times the size of the dot child

my children are in the ocean
a wave comes and rolls one
he stands
his hair dreadlocked clumps of sand
the next wave he will stumble out screaming
holding his side rubbed raw
a half shell that sliced him
we don't leave.
i pull his tiny frame
to salt
and watch his blood dilute
the sting
he is numb within ten minutes
asks *does good medicine always burn?*
i think of that for days.

dry drowning is what we call
hours later at dinner when your child is under an ocean
that you can not see
the salt could kill them
gulps of chemically imbalanced blood
i think of thirty-six more ways as the next wave rises before them
and they dive into the soft belly of her
like i taught them
so the white mouth
that carries the teeth never hits
nor her tongue that folds all under

i am the one that taught my babies to swim
their legs strangling my waist
i'm the one that bent my knees
letting the water slowly climb up our backs
how i waited for the next rise and blew in their face
so they inhaled

then ducked our bodies under together
a coyote once took off with my little dog
but the end of her tie-out jolted its run
taking only the skin off her back before
i hit it with the side of my fist
i am every second aware that my children aren't tied
to anything in this abyss
that these creatures know to pull low
to drown air bodies
making skin a specimen in the largest jar of preservative there is

she's as endless as space
the cold deoxygenated black between stars
they can't officially name any sea creature extinct
because a large percentage has never been seen
do you hear me?
megalodon may still exist.
we've seen the giant squid wash up
and blue whales with bodies like cruise ships
eyes the size of soccer balls
not to mention the series of recorded ocean sounds
that no one can identify
one that sounds like a train
one like the name *julia* called out over and over
i once sat at a bar in kaua'i beside
the best shark photographer in the world
he asked me if i knew how my whitefish was sourced
i didn't ask how he lost his leg

this is not a warning or maybe it is
what is safety? an illusion.
we drop our children off at school and some kid brings a gun
we get in cars that crush like a miller light can
under a steel-toed boot
and then there's cancer
i was barely 12 with stage four melanoma

i know there are some parents that say
they don't allow their kids inside the unknown
but isn't it all?
this body of water merely another world
i have brought them into
and taught them to swim
knowing well i may not be able to save them

my daughter has started
folding her lips
over her teeth when she smiles
there has been a divorce
cross-country move
sometimes when i remember how i tore their world
my shoulders drop
when i feel her eyes
i straighten as if i were a god
it's such a lie so i drive her
to the top of the canyon
open your mouth i say
are you angry?!
god damn it say it.
i'm pissed off i say.
she's 8 and laughs.
me too mommy
what else?
i'm so sad she says
me too i say. i'm so sad.
i want to pull her back into me
bury her under my wing.
there was a bantam hen on my farm
i found her one morning in the field
with the top half of her body gone
skin eaten off her back
sixchicks untouched beneath her wings
if only i could have stayed in one place
when it came for my back
she could have walked out to sun the next morning
emerged untouched from under a body still warm

instead i walk her to the top of the canyon
i count down
and we produce a sound
a brutal tear
a ballooning of rib
a ripping ache
the sound of the hen in the night

our voices between red thirst and desert plant
nothing swallows us into the landscape
our sound drowns in each other's sky
i know this won't always be a good deal for me
she often roars things i don't like to hear
her words make marks in the wall
her brother's arm
last week she stomped two ikea miles
twenty feet behind me slapping her little boots to the floor
i know i've birthed a wild thing
i know what i'm doing
making sure she knows she breathes fire.
i know i'll not come out unscathed.
i know this won't always be a good deal for me.
i make it anyway.

i too have loved men and not one of them could hold it
can i hold the immense waving sheet kissing marin bay?
dusk of softest glass
the wet that splits heaven
i pull my head back to yell at the steep of redwoods
the tallest locked-mouth empaths
do i deserve this?
i'm no fool.
i know what i am to a thousand upon thousand years
jersey cow eyelashes
the bird of a luna moth
devastating beauty
emerging without a mouth
to live a single day
it has never been if he deserved my love
it is and has always been that in the morning
a burning woman 109 times wider than earth
will rise a hopeful artist
with ready wrists
and paint the world awake
the point is that i loved.
and my god i loved.

the day we moved in
there was a 9-year-old rattlesnake in the kitchen
a foot away from my son
coiled. hissing. demanding we leave.
i know her age because there was a shovel propped against the wall
and i now have the rattle.

at four a.m. my daughter woke me to say a mouse crawled up her shirt
and out the neck. there was a period at the end of this. a fact.
she went back to sleep.

i sleep alone knowing i never sleep alone.

there are no screens. i leave the windows open. we swallow marine
layer and forget meals. we haven't been sick a day since we moved in.

we have all been turned inside out.

this morning i watched four spiders the size of my fist climb through
a crack in the steamed window and up the shower wall.
one kept sliding down. i picked her up by the leg
and put her eye level with the rest.

the coyotes here don't starve or mange in winter
they eat.
its shoulders roll slow and eyes knife my little dog.
its back scrapes the height of the dining room table in the yard.
when i throw up my arms it doesn't run.

i have a wood stove. i burn from a stack never stacked. the kids climb
it and chew the yellow flowers and mallow behind.
i boil water on top for tea. the water i wash dishes and shower under
i watch run down the hill. i collect rainwater under two roof's
edges in bins for the garden. there isn't much left of the garden. the
pheasants left tomatoes and rosemary and the marigolds. i can't not
drown or burn the flowers here. they too are living for the poetry.

the crow family is as big as hawks. when they land on the tin roof
we duck inside. they know we are below them.

i cut their toenails on tuesdays on the concrete floor. i scrub
sand from their scalps. we are never clean. mary flew in.
she said *we're low key dirty.* i say *we're all just dirt in denial.*

someone is always itching.

men with beard oil and $3200 vintage boots kiss me and tell
me they taste the ocean. i taste nothing. i've drowned them all.

the rattle that sits in my window makes me weak in my arms.
as an apology i drive the next one in a rubbermaid without a
lid to the shadows of the canyon. she looks at me like she knows
i'm not sorry. she looks at me like she knows if she got close to
the boy with my eyes i'd do it again.

she looks at me like i'm a wild thing too.

i hope you're bored as hell.

i hope the whole time she's talking you think
the word fuck with four u's.
i hope the whole time she's talking you think
a loaded gun in the bedside table

i hope she knows nothing of adrienne rich.
or shakespeare's man lover
or that mute swans mate for life.

i hope she calls it her yoni
and takes her sound bowls
on your vacations

i hope she dms you atticus
some shit like
you have always been a tree!
i hope she's gluten intolerant
and snacks on rice patties and microgreens.

i hope
going from me to
answering your favorite holiday
you have taken up hard drugs
god i hope you're shooting up in the bathroom
going to house parties every weekend
on mdma! the kind you drink in pink broth
to forget purgatory exists

i hope you do frog poison to forget me!
and your eyes swell shut
i hope you sit in a circle of puke buckets
and grandmother ayahuasca comes down the mountain
just to tell you you're a fucking idiot.

i hope every letter you don't write me
clots in your dorsal metacarpal vein
until you lose the feeling in your writing hand

dear god i don't mean it.

i hope you don't have a cough
that your neck isn't sore when you wake
i hope you only wake to good dreams
still reach to touch leaves
and always find the kitchen light when you need a drink

i hope you think you hurt me
even though i don't
want you to know
even though i definitely
want you to know
you hurt me.

i hope that every day
pretending you don't love me
is just you
really really
good at pretending

and i hope
you get worse
at it soon.

i'm sorry but you are not my man

my man has a beard
tastes like tobacco
and wears a denim shirt to your wedding
my man has more scars than you
one from a chainsaw
one from a mean dog
and a pollock of sunspots

there is a morning i catch my man
taking a spider web off the ceiling with tweezers
transporting it like one of those trailer homes
on a flatbed truck
and sticking it perfectly intact to the porch

my man would go in debt before he'd let me pay for half of dinner

one time i straddle my man
and put mascara on him in bed
and tell him how very pretty he his

my man laughs at reiki healers
with porn lisps that channel god
he once grabbed my ass and said
no woman on a juice fast
can fuck like you fuck!

my man says *you are not afraid are you?*
of anything are you?
and picks weeds and puts them in a vase

my man is a little meaner than you
reads frank bidart
and says things like
garbage is spiritual

my man calls people with giant crystals
rapists of the earth
and has renamed
my ex-boyfriends
plastic
and *tesla*
and *little bitch*

i tell my man the story
about my grandfather crying
after running over a kitten
with his mower
and my man cries too

when the canyon is on fire
he gets the poems out first
and cozy cat
my man runs back in for my grandmother's hanky

my man calls me sunday
my man calls me live wire
my man calls me proof
of the great flood

my man gets road head
just for being beautiful
and says *i'm going to drive off this canyon woman!*
says *what a way to die!*

i wake with my man inside me
my man is an earth god with
hands that i named brazil
and the cold war

sometimes i get a text
that says *mama you've been on my mind*
sometimes i get a text that says
the freckle on your lip is my god

one time in his thirst for me
he tears my favorite shirt
my man hand sews it

my man grew up poor
my man can make a meal out of a potata

one time i look at him and i say
i think of you when i read the words tender buttons
one time i tell him i'd put on my old skin
just to die with him
one time i ask how it
feels living in my subclavian?
and he says *warm.*
can you believe it?
my man says *warm.*

the want that lives in me
for you to want me
is stronger and more terrible
than anything i could see or unsee
if it ever broke free
it would do what great terrible things do
stop the sea from pulling under
pour dams of concrete between
wield knives from cafeteria trays
handles made out of it's own hair
then sharpen itself against
those concrete walls
in splitting seas
it could teach pain to pain
humans have done worse
marrying the men that follow the ones like you
type of men that call home on their drive home
and you don't give a fuck
that they are calling home on their drive home
that sleep beside me while i think
of nothing but running down a mountain in the dark with you.
the photo under my bed
that my daughter will find too late
ask of too late
straighten the corners and then pocket too late
a bird flies over me
its shadow falls over my body
and then leaves
this something inside me could
close one eye
shoot it from the sky
tear off its wings
while it was still alive
it's been done before
with less ripping
through the letters
the cheese knife you put in my stocking
holes and holes and holes in chests
the text i tried to claw out of my phone

you telling me you don't know
insects that are born to only live a day
your mouth breathing into mine
still this want for you
to want me
will never
pull at your freckled hands
god on the eighth day made it that way
so we couldn't live forever
and this is why
i pulled the curtains down
at 8 years old
just to hide under them
but this want
could tie my hair around the handle
and it could press its blade to the place
my lung and heart and muscle caved around you
it could carve your home from me
it could.
but it will never be able to bring you back
inside my kitchen
the hydrangeas still in plastic
the bag of oysters
you handing me
a stack of cookbooks
you chose for me

go fuck yourself.

go fuck yourself with your fundamentalist church lies!
go fuck yourself doggie on club mile-high!

go fuck yourself deep with a bde!
go fuck yourself shallow with a micropenie
a sandy ass crack at malibu state beach!

go fuck yourself drunk on vodka crans low vibe!
go fuck yourself dalai lama chanting mountainside!
go fuck yourself shakespeare
may your moans rhyme!
in perfect iambic pentameter time!

go fuck yourself disappointing shower sex wall!
go fuck yourself in chains
north korean prison stall!

fuck yourself lsd
colors unseen!
go fuck yourself john mayer
a c o u s t i c a l l y

go fuck yourself your 13-year-old wet dream
hell record yourself fucking yourself
and watch it on tv!

fuck yourself baptized and on your knees!
fuck yourself threesome with adam and eve!
then go fuck yourself
lil nas x style the devil's dirty tease

go fuck yourself gay
fuck yourself straight
fuck yourself while psychic in chinatown reads your fate

go fuck yourself watching *my girl*
anaphylactic shock! chased by the bees!
fuck yourself in airbnb cleaning fees!

fuck yourself in furry handcuffs
fuck yourself until you fuck yourself free
and with your dirty hand
continue to reach! and reach! and reach
but honey
i am vibing way too high
for you to ever
ever
fuck with me.

when we read that a woman killed a man
we see her torture.
we see her sleeping beside him.
we see her bringing him nyquil.
the sleeves she ironed the last thing she saw
before she lost consciousness
fuck. this says there were children.
daughters. you know exactly what you are thinking.
life in prison tasted better than seeing what she saw again
we hear this and see her bruised invisible line crossed
we hear this and
we see her shakily loading the gun
we hear this and
we see her finally deciding to live.

there is a reason when you hear a man killed a woman
you think he didn't even know her
he wanted inside her and then cut her up so small
he could chew her
stalk her tie her chop her drown her bag her burn her
silence her
silence her
silence her

do you not think there is a reason we think this?
our bodies know where violence lives.
our bodies know the patriarchal chambers that keep it.
don't you dare ignore instinct.
don't you dare ignore statistics.
don't you dare ignore the truth.
that we all fucking know
that nobody will fucking speak aloud
that they kill us to silence us.
we kill them to survive.

my daughter finds an injured dragonfly
i tell her what i shouldn't
i tell her it will starve slowly
unless. unless. and ask permission
she begs me not to.
i promise.
when she leaves i take a rock to it.
and cover it in sand.

my mother tells a story about a litter of kittens
one that was born making the worst sound in the world
how my father did what she could not
cupped it in his hand
hit it in the head with a hammer

when the baby the size of my thumb
heart stopped beating inside of me
i woke in the night and knew
they said it could take weeks
me carrying my dead child. weeks.
i kept getting the alerts on my phone
he has rubbery fingers. he has eyelids. a bend in his tubelike arm.
i shook. i leaned against walls
i muffled my noise into a college hoodie in my closet.
though my mother said *let god do it in his time.*
i signed on the line
uterine ablation is burning your rich red to black
a dead baby pulled from its home
or its home stripped of its grave.
but *its home is me* i wanted to scream!
my home is me.

when the man i love became ice
i showed up at his house at one a.m.
my suitcase still in the back of the uber
the door was locked
i scaled his back fence and scraped my ribs
and knocked on his bedroom window
didn't tell him i was bleeding beneath my shirt

i knew as soon as he opened the door
i had scared him against a wall i could not climb
he wanted me to let it die
quietly. and in its sleep.
and step and step and step away.
i do not know this way
and got on the plane holding my side.

there are people that can carry a slow death
that can give space to the dying of things
i am not one of these.
there are people who can turn and let it be
let love sit lonely and not speak
tell me how to walk away from suffering
when i know prayer is the fire
when i know sometimes my best offering is the rock.

i found my old diary tonight
a brokenness i had forgotten
pen pressed so deep it punctured page
i ran my fingers over my words
and there inside ridges black
i found a little girl
desperate
for someone to save her
desperate
for the very woman
i have become.

you're so hot.

you're so hot i want to travel west in a covered wagon across your lips and put up stake in your right dimple. i want to get typhoid and name my 104 fever your stupid hot name.

you're so hot i learn electric guitar. make an 80's hair band. our first album titled *your eyelashes.*
i go on tour. i pour honey down my throat. i scream about your hands. i hit every note.

you're so hot i'm facetiming you talking about pad see ew and tracing my collarbones. you're so hot i'm facetiming you about pad see ew and my shirt is off. you're so hot i'm facetiming you about pad see ew more naked than an acoustic chris cornell song.

you're so hot i demand you to screenshot.

you're so hot i rename you fist full of sand.
i rename you white part of the flame.
i rename you lion belly in sahara sun.

you're so hot i'm angry.
i break all my grandmother's china.
i grit my teeth.
i grind them half off to tiny piles of tooth dust.

you're so hot i take you to the sedalia state fair
just to burn my mouth on funnel cake oil
just to lick powdered sugar off your beard.

you're so hot you baby talk to my cat.

you're so hot we have to turn to each other and say *we have to finish now* and still don't finish. the word finish has never been invented. the word finish has been retroactively retracted from webster. the word finish still lives in the interplanetary black velvet void where you take me
when. we. don't. finish.

you're so hot in your fucking stocking
hat i bite off my lower lip.

you're so hot i drive you onion pit stink in a gold el dorado
off-road mojave with the plan to break down with the plan
to drink your sweat.

you're so hot my dick that i don't have is hard. you're so hot
my dick that i don't have is out like one of those idiot boys
in college you're so hot i've unzipped my pants my dick out
that i don't have saying whatcha gonna do about this. huh.
you have to help me out here babe.

you're so hot i see a photo of your hands and arch. you're
so hot i see the smallest vein in your worst arm and i'm
fisting the pillow.

you're so hot i've burned the eggs
again. i have stopped praying.
i now believe in hell.
i take up smoking cigarettes with the birth defect labels in
europe.

you're so hot so help me mary
or buddha or mama ocean or frank ocean
so help me god!

you're so hot.

listen up p.
i don't want to meet your mama.
i want to meet your night psychic and drive the devil into hell.
i want to ride below your crupper.
take your horizontal refreshment. pogue my hone.
i want the chemical of you.
i want to sit behind you in science class p.
i want your mg your fe on a not-so-periodic-table.
let's skip prom and swallow virginity in the back of your toyota
truck. more tongue p. rug burns p. listen up p i need a wedding date
in portugal. tickets are cheap p.
let's throw away our deodorant.
i want your onion and salt and deep seed.
i want your man sounds. your held breath.
i want your brown legs x-ing and x-ing my brown legs. i wanna get
real confused about whose legs are whose legs. listen up p.
drive to me.
i want the neighbors complaining.
i'm not the wedding p. i'm the bachelor party p. tequila. the real
good stuff p. call me clase azul. you can take me over and over again.
maybe we'll get a little sick p.
then you can go to your models their 90's bones and one-liner poetry
and i'll go back to men that don't live in me
and pay for my dinner p
and he'll kiss me in the parking lot of cafe havana too
and i'll wish it was you
so listen up p we have this perfectly terrible summer and you still
want to kiss me with your freedom p then hang me by my neck over
the edge. so keep me there.
listen up p i want you with a side of the old pier and giant kelp
i want the 95% unexplored sea
i want you in an abandoned house
graffiti evidence on our hands
let's get arrested p. cuss out the cops. put up your dukes. run.
let's run p.
then sleep outside in some cave freeze our asses off p
i want you between your leaning canvas and plants
on your concrete countertops p
i want you on your dirty office couch
i want your awkward hammock sex

knees by ears by elbows by femurs by
stay hydrated p. 26.2 marathon me
paint me like one of your french girls
my arm over my head i'm trying not to laugh but you're
spending lots of time on that nipple.
don't worry i'm going to act like i forgot your middle name.
don't worry p
i'm gonna not stare too long.

listen up p
i know what happened last summer
but we can do this
we're grown-ups now
nobody is falling in love this time

i kiss the argentinian
on the beach in tulum
he is all lips
and golden and
no anchor in him.
i say *teach me a word.*
piola
he chooses
a rope.

then lights the j beneath his shirt and
catches a small fire and laughs
he points at the horizon.
the finality he calls it
and i could fall in love with him
trade all my wicked art
take the pills he hands me
but i will not.

you are 25 i say.

on the back of his motorcycle i count the palms that are bowing
and whisper into his neck
something he will never hear.

call me in 20 years.

after your ten-year marriage and divorce hearing
after the first weekend without your children
you spend fetaled in bed
after you buy your first drill and after you rust it from fixing up
your canyon shack with rats
call me after you lose that home.
and after you forsake your religion
after your mother tries to sue you.
call me after you can not pay your rent and you feed
the kids cans of spaghettios

call me after the lover in florence
the french gypsy on the dirt road in todos santos
call me after you fall in love for the first time
and say *never again!*
then call me after you do it again.
call me after the cancer diagnosis
and they cut into your leg
call me after you have begged god for another chance with
the one that won't give you another chance
call me after you've done ayahuasca in the jungle
and aliens kill your ego and inject your brain with love
call me after the canyon is on fire and you watch it burn
call me after you sleep tangled in sweat with your children
the windows open
your only fan on all of you.

i'm not saying you have to live my life to love me.
what i'm saying is
beneath the pacific ocean in the southern end
of the mariana trench there is a home 12,100 feet deep

i'm saying i bet there is a heart there too
of some creature swimming alone.

i'm saying i'm placing bets
it is the tenderest in all the world
and to reach it
to dive that deep and touch it
you'd have to be too.

*i did it world i manifested the love of my life
and he's 2825.3 miles away*

the kids. no one is going anywhere.
cruel joke universe.

i think i will go to an abraham hicks retreat
raise both my dirty fingers in the air
yell *fuck you universe*
and be escorted out by some hippie in white
that i will try to fight

i think i'll go to a sound bath meditation
and right when she hits the $500 rose quartz bowl
i'll stand up and yell
fuck you to hell and back universe

i think i'll go to your ex-boyfriend's girlfriend's yoga class
stand up during savasana
and yell
fuck you. you fucking fuck universe

for the next ten years i will date men
that i kind of hate and love you.

everytime i'm with him
the man i kind of hate
because he's not you
i will imagine you seeing us
from across the street
and move my hair out of my face like you do
what i want him to do
what he will never do

the man i kind of hate
because he's not you
standing and watching
without a chance

sad but not really sad
ego-sad which is different sad
and is the sad of most men
that will love me without loving me
because they are not
you loving me

i imagine you saying to him
robot! how dare you not call her lark!
how dare you not send her a painted mug!
how dare you be a plastic sack
a pericardium
the wrapping of a heart
and not the heart

you listen to me
my hands are fisting your shirt
i've pushed you against the locker
you just listen to me.
i wanted to keep you.
i wanted to keep you for my whole life
i wanted to make them all watch
and grow sick of us and
our slow moving fingers
you just listen to me!
if i'm not the one to love you
you better make damn sure
you are kissed between your eyes.

damn sure she knows about blue #00f5ff
the ol' brass bed
or leave her in the horrible restaurant
where you don't share your meal
leave her in the middle of a whole foods parking lot
leave her crying into her reusable grocery sacks

unlike me i swear to you she will find someone else
unlike me she will not meet your ghost in every poem
clawing in her wrist

unlike me she will be just fine
just fine without you.

in every life
you sit on our bed
made of moss or the one i carved you from the trunk
with my daddy's knife
and oh i love you.

in every life
your friends are vampire bats
i squint an eye
shoot them from the sky

in every life
you kiss me at wave break
and 2178 miles of ocean catches fire

in every life
i think of you
taking off the necklaces
and i cry.

in every life
i buy you a farm
plant you a strawberry patch
fill the bowls with heavy cream and sugar

we take the airstream to portland
johnny and june
and you give me a hand-poked tattoo

in every life i wrap you in a cocoon
wield you a sword from blacksmith iron
roll the poems into glass bottles
and the scrolls lay undead in every sea

in every life
i am robbed.
and you fall down the rabbit hole

in every life you tackle me to smell my b.o.

we put on carole king records
stop shaving our legs
and i take your shirt off the hanger
press it to my face

in every life
you are arrested in a foreign land
and i am maniacal with armed men
chewing cotton wool

in every life
i find you at the masquerade
rip off your glittered mask
and throw it in the fire.

in every life loving me is a sin
so they bury us in an unnamed grave
they bury us on the pyre sent to sea!
they bury us in the pyramids
fill our tombs with ten thousand scarab beetles of jade
in every life my last request
that they wrap our legs together
while we sleep

my words are spells
so i write in my blackest ink you won't leave me on a tuesday
or on our beachwalk handing me the broken shell
you will not leave me at lax terminal 7
or on a past life torture table
in a folded grained photo
one in a pocket so long it has become cotton
you will not leave me in a coffee-stained letter
not even a sickening beautiful one
like only you would write
you will not leave me for a yoga teacher that can do pigeon
or a british jesus dj that puts spirulina and broccoli in smoothies

you will not leave me for actual jesus or dalai lama
or something ayahuasca told you
you won't leave me for quoting the fucking holistic psychologist
or for a tuluminati flat brimmed hat
you will not leave me because the church hates us
or because i have children that fight in the backseat

you will not leave me for less of a poem
or a duller knife
or a tongue of lesser thirst

you lay there a well in your throat
the deep kind of blue that you know
i have already swallowed
you lay there and you are what i can not undo.
you lay there and i know by now the lie of forever
you lay there legs scissored and my air is small
you lay there and tu eres mi alma.
you lay there i can not unknow the one thing that i know.
there is no mercy here.
you lay here. right here.
and i miss you
i miss you already.

i want to be in a jane austen novel with you

i want to wear gauzy white and
let my curls fall loose and
dirty my hem to run miles to you
in my laced up boots
and you to call me an *obstinate headstrong girl*
i want to see you in candlelight
and outwit all the men that talk to you

i want to go ribbon shopping
and buy a half yard of the deep red velvet
and let you tie me up by my wrists

there is a dance at netherfield tonight
i want to ask you for the first
during the first i want to ask for the second
during the second
the third and

i want to clear the floor
i want everyone gossiping about two women
i want our carriage flying home in the rain
and then i want to tent the goose down over our heads

i want to wake at dawn
and play the piano forte
so it echoes and ripples your still sleep
i want you to
descend the carved grand staircase
with the nightsticks looking at me soft-lidded
and perfectly and incandescently happy

i want you to demand we ride the horses in the rain
like you would and

i want you to get a fever
that makes me pace outside your room

and insist we immediately leave for a bath to heal
and then i want to open all the windows to sea air
i want to press my lips to your forehead
and lay beside you and play with your hair
play with your hair
until all of your life returns

when i imagine my pain

i imagine an auditorium
a red curtain parting
me coming silently
to the edge of the stage
with this ache so heavy i can barely lift
a black two-ton rock
my stepfather is inside
my ex-husband.
my first love at the super 8 as i drove away
my own mother forgetting me.
my brother. oh my baby brother.
the miscarriage
politics. war. religion. cancer. credit unions.
court dates.

the people are afraid.
what will she do with this?
i hoist it above my head and stand shaking
and then i do the unthinkable
i throw it as high as i can above them all
they don't know yet
all the love inside me is around it
like a spell
all my prayers
intangible cries
the sum of the night
and right at the height
when it could cause horrific damage
my pain
turns to
the softest
pink
petals
floating down slow
landing on every human
that came to my show

a little girl catches two handfuls
and raises them above her head
she is my daughter.

her hands full of my love
her hands full of my love

i want to carve a thousand tiny wooden birds and paint them in
horrible neon colors and put them on your porch when you open
the door

you. the type of magnificent creature that drives slower so the ant
doesn't fall off the hood of the car

i want to gauge out my eyes with my own thumbs

you look at me.
bury me in a rotating truck of wet concrete!
you kiss me
your mouth is the sea of galilee and i'm floating in your salt
your mouth the last mango
and what the prayers of silent monks are made of
you magnificent frigate bird
you painted lady
you monkey in the jungle with the biggest balls

how dare you make me this weak!
how dare you make me want to tie on a cape and climb on the roof!

i'll take the hot oil and the rack!
beat the drum i am walking toward the guillotine!

i want to take a school bus through your capillaries.
i want to shrink into a subatomic particle and crawl inside
you and picnic under your alveolar trees.

if i lived in your rivers would you dance?

you touch my hair and i order a reposado
and drop poison into it from my necklace

i want to crush the snake that gets close to you
beneath my heel like a caravaggio painting
holding your jesus hands
i spend all day
with my hand between my legs.
i am the runt of the litter.

take a hammer to my forehead!
i want to go to therapy as
the most codependent couple in history.
i am the glomerulus and you are the kidney
and i filter the drugs you inject in us.
you make me drunk.
you make me vomit in my hair.
you make me fall off curbs and
dance
and dance
and dance.

you talk about your exes that want you
i want to rub myself in red meat
and dive into piranha waters

i want to make a balloon out of your smile
break the record in the guinness book for
the biggest balloon in the macy's thanksgiving parade
i want it to be made of your perfect white teeth space
and your perfect fucking lips
i want to make your balloon unpoppable.
even as i cut the string.
even as it gets close to the sun.
even as i squint as it gets smaller and smaller
and i stand on the sidewalk like a pathetic kid
and cry and cry and cry.

i hate how much i want you.

and it's not even time for me to leave
my bags are packed
the car is coming to get me
and you are already so far away
and there has never been anything more true in me than
i don't want to leave you.

behind every great man artist
is a woman that brought him lunch on little floral plates
while he chewed on his fucking pencil.

french for dusk is
entre chien et loup
between dog and wolf
and you want me to make a man a sandwich?

the human i am with must feed themselves
and that says more than i am trying to say.

in this box of pens there is no kitchen!
in this box of pens the oven burns everything
in this box of pens i offer you a paper map to get lost
i offer you a river that will take you home
in this box of pens i offer you birdsong
sexsong. jungle leaves that
fall slow and make boats

there are women that enjoy cooking for you but all i can think of is
where all the masterpieces go when chopping?
the metaphors lost by poet in aprons
hands full of spatula
the color that gathers in gutters
while they sauté his fucking meat

listen to me
for the next several thousand years
a woman belongs in the kitchen
writing a poem
while her man
brings her a perfectly seasoned salad

listen to me
i want you to never stand in front of a da vinci
a picasso

a page of flaubert
a fucking bernini ever again
ever again
and not praise
the silent artist
the woman
that fed him.

may my children never read this.

one night in rome a band
bought me a beer
the lead singer was wearing a shirt
of screaming kittens.
so i said *kiss me.*
he pulled me into an alley in trastevere
tasted like marlboros
and stuck my finger in his mouth
sucked off my snake ring.
and put it on his pinkie
(so i took him back to my airbnb)

we were kissing on the couch
and i said *what is that.*
(hard down to his knee)
he said *look and see!*

and i unzipped and it wouldn't come out
so i stripped his levi's down to his knees
and said

that is the biggest i've ever seen!
that is not real!
and *what. what.*
are you kidding me?

and i inspected it.
and laughed so hard i cried
and told him *my whole life god had lied!*

and measured it around both of my hands

and he got very very happy
but i said
that is not going near me

and gave it a sweet little goodbye kiss on its head
i'm very tired! and very drunk! i said

you should go!
but he said *i'm too drunk to drive home!*
and i said *call a car!*
he said *the streets are too narrow!*
he said *it's too far to go!*

and i said *then walk! you have two legs*
hell you have three!
and he made prayer hands
it hanging to his knee.
the man begged
have mercy on me!

and i said *i have one rule for rome*
no man stays the night!
all of them go home!

go go! get up and go!
he bent his head and walked out slow
and the next morning
i realized he had my ring!

and i said *damn it! what a thing!*
and walked outside empty hand
but oh the witch i am!

there was a folding table set up
outside the door
of all sizes of gold snake rings!
nothing more.

and i said *this universe is wildly fun.*

(and chose the
slightly larger
than average one.)

good morning.
the sun is 93 million miles away
her light takes eight minutes
to find you each day
you are on purpose.

i keep saying over and over
i'm sorry but i have to go now
you are not my person

i am being stupid
loyal to a two-thousand-year-old promise
loyal to the night we fell asleep in the stable
everything we had in that wooden box you buried under the floor

hell you may not even be in this galaxy!
you're on 554 lightway
two million suns as an indigo energy body
that i would still know
by temperature alone
the speed you travel down
my pharynx
to set a little fire

you should know by now
i am set on you.
you should know by now
i kick the flank in the war.

you should know by now i've become
a flock of birds that turn noonday to night
you should know i've become
a flock of birds circling for you

are you watching this go down?

he was never you.
you'd call me *a burning sea.*
you'd title my book.
you'd put your dukes up.
you'd say *you best leave her alone!*

how long will you wait?

i'm going to stick my tongue in your ear and like it.
i am going to buy you a gas station trucker hat
to find out what you look like in a gas station trucker hat
i'm going to watch you hang up on your mother
and say *that was an asshole thing to do.*
i'm going to take a photo of you standing calf deep in a body of water
i'm going to put mascara on you. call you a pretty thing.
i'm going to piss you off real bad.
i'm already not sorry.

excuse me. we need to fly to missoura.
you need to sit on the porch while my father plays guitar
excuse me. i picked this honeysuckle so your office becomes july.
excuse me i have a jar of lightning bugs for you.
take off the lid.

excuse me. i am getting creased
on the side of my smile
it's time to climb out of a case of paints!
out of a baroque chair leg!
excuse me it's time to get on the right planet.
excuse me
crawl out of the damn primordial sludge
into a body.
a body that has legs and
run to me.

last night i walked in the bar you were playing
and when you saw me with him you breathed hot into the mic
and sang *nothing compares to you* and i thought of how
the landlord said he never saw so many marks in the walls
we tore off the doorframe getting the couch out
it was the last thing we'd carry and so heavy
you kicked it and said *it fucking came in here fine*
and it did. it all did. until it ate and made love and screamed itself
weak in the dusty corners and woke me the night i found you
on our linoleum with an empty bottle of woodford
and our only kitchen knife and i thought you might kill my god
and grabbed the blade with my bare hand
and it's true he could never make me bleed like you
when you sang those lines your eyes didn't leave mine
and you weren't even holding a knife this time
but we both knew
i would leave cut through.

you can't go to a kindergarten teacher after me

you can't go to a butter knife
and bleed hot and clean

you're a stones groupie
at a britney concert

you tripped on ayahuasca
and drove straight to a sephora

you walked out of the louvre
into a hobby lobby

you went from alanis
writing jagged little pill down her arm
to sitting across the table
from a sunday school teacher at a ruth's chris

garth is singing whiskey to wine
while you do her reiki and swear it's a great time!

she says that she's witchy!
and that her labradorite on her tv stand brings her power
a great sedona find!
(i do all this shit with my mind)

she's calabasas
i'm the cliffs of big sur
where i rolled a perfectj
you know how tight
(you know how tight)
you check into a god-awful hyatt for the night
to starve on her love
to starve on her light

i know while she's sleeping
you lock the bathroom door
turn on the shower
and pull up the videos of me

fool you should have known
you can't go to a kindergarten teacher
after me

the thing about jesus is he could see another dimension
the wet leper baby-skinned
heavy nets.

give that man a fucking paint brush!
some papyrus!
a woman that calls him
on his bullshit
knows her way up a neck

hey jesus.
nobody walks anymore in venice
they're all on roller skates
filming each other.
there's your first line jesus.

hey jesus
peel me like a potata
hey jesus
endless disease blah blah
wreck my plans
fill the baskets with fish
leftovers stinking in the sun.
hey jesus
do your god-damned job!
pin me like you know how!
stack my feet
i'm giving you
one nail.

god is a woman
and like every woman
has millions of years of men
speaking for her

she doesn't back your president
or load your guns
or make lab disease for your pharma money

she chooses to speak only
through the head bent reception of baby bird mouths
venus flytraps closing on winged things
lover's shallow breath.
whale songs. placenta.
a hurricane or two when she needs a stretch
god doesn't back your president
or load your guns
she digests your bread
gives urge to kiss
god is in labor
birthing newborn fists at every corner of sun
folding the dead into her soil
god is a woman
like every woman
has millions of years of men
speaking for her
a billion voices
she could drown
with one storm

one tornado i lived through got the house.
it sounds like a train you are not on
you are tied like cartoon dynamite beneath the tracks
though you are in the cellar lined with shaking cans of salsa
pickled peppers

the house was still standing
which was confusing to the neighbors
but the windows were in the carpet
the roof pulled off in all the places
you can not see from the road

some people are hit by storms like this
they wear their red bottom shoes
botox their lines smooth
shingles glued in all the places you can see
the windows unbroken in the front

we hang photos over the water stains
but we've all lived under the same dark sky
and some have water gathering in pools in the ceiling
and break behind the wheel of their tesla
or in the comment section of your poem

but tell me who hasn't picked up glass with their bare hands?
who hasn't ran for a bucket?
who hasn't made tiny repairs day by day
just to remember the home that lives
inside our bodies?

it happened like i thought it might
i run into you
years after the night
i hated you
because i could not
share you.

it's mortifying wanting someone so much.
i reread the letters and didn't sleep for four days.

i wanted to wrap you in the comforter
and beat you with the frying pan.

i wanted to ice-skate across a frozen sea with you.

i wanted to read the book backwards
in every language i don't know.

i wanted to have your baby just to kiss her more
where she looked like you.

i wanted to bathe in every creek in the world
for you to bring me a pan
to rinse my hair.

i wanted to stay in the furnace until we turned gold.

fuck me and all my wrong lovin'.

(the man with me was not my boyfriend)
i almost yelled it!
i almost fashioned a whip!
jesus style flipped the tables!

i almost said right then and there
in front of her
i still love you.

instead *you taught me how*
pointed to the oysters.

she said *you have never taught me!*
he's never taught me how!

how's the writing? you said
but it sounded like *how's the rotting*
same.
i had forgotten your accent
when you hugged me i tried to crawl inside

a 17th century skinning alive

when i found out you asked out my rich friend
in your writing class
i almost filled my pockets with rocks
and walked into the sea

i told everyone you were gay.
i told everyone you were sad.
i was more gay.
i was more sad.

they say you only know these things after.
so i must have loved you.
i must have really loved you.

i want one more letter.

you could tell me
how impossible i was.
and then call me beauty.

i could tell you about the da vinci paintings that
are trapped in a wall.

i could tell you about the man
that has stood on top of a hot air balloon.
he brought a folding chair to stand on
it was pepto-pink i'd say.

i talked to the woman with you for a while
but it was as if i was talking to air
telling the priest my sins
while god watched leaning against the wall
staring at me like the great mistake i am

as if we were in a world of robots
as if the night you hiked up my dress
we were given the
last two throbbing hearts on earth
and reminded again.

and how terrible
how terrible
to know
something like that.

i will not fix you
but i will name you perfect inside your pain
point out sparrows and sidewalk weeds
and when your fingers are in mine
i'll raise them to my lips
and watch as you heal in your bones

i should now admit
i once made a fake account
just to talk to you once more
there is nothing crueler
than to be cold to who we love most
why do we do it?

why.

it had been months
i had not a word from you
i was spending hundreds
i didn't have
for psychics to tell me
you still loved me

the account took me weeks
i built a believable following
took some photos of bourbon cabinet
at a friend's house
the man went to nyu.
and asked about your recipes.

god i am crazy.

every time you responded so quickly
i wanted to die
you talked to him the way
you talked to the homeless man on 5th avenue
bent to ask about his birds.

i have never wanted to crawl inside anything
like i wanted your cage.

it was like that horrible movie
i was channing tatum
you were in that car wreck
amensia made you forget me.
and i was punching holes in walls
i'd never patch

you were so kind to him.
explaining the curry.
it was all god's sickest trick.

i flew across the world once to walk where you once walked.

i thought about yelling *how dare you jesus i'm starving!*
and you gave the fish to full-bellied strangers.

none of it made any sense
like the time you cheated me in my dream
and i spent the whole morning crying into your chest

it was all a waste.
a terrible idea.
i deleted the account while you were still typing
something like
of course, anytime man!

horrible. the touching you
without touching you.

almost worse than never
touching you again.

blame my angels
quirky bitches
bringing me jean jackets
garage sale art. buicks that won't start.
beautiful men to break my heart
they never taught me to behave
guess they were busy
making damn sure i was brave

when i was 7 i watched my mother
26 divorced and barely one hundred pounds
give $25 for a dresser for our clothes
and without looking side to side
she hugged it wide
arms shaking
and she lifted it herself into the pickup bed.
and this. this is all i have ever needed to see.

god still comes to visit
the devil she left in me
snags my lowest cut silk
we dance until morning
after we smoke my good stuff
talk of sex and what we read
she says i need to lose the man
and reminds me of my dreams

you know the headline
human raises wild animal
and then tastes the power
of undomesticated holiness
and the bear he calls baby
or alligator allocated to the bathtub
the tiger he taught to sit pretty
to stay. balance a sunhat
flares its gums. head low stalks
around the coffee table
then strings the captor's bowels
across the living room carpet
of some city apartment
i too am a wild warm blood
and will only be disrespected so long
i too know well the strength of my jaw
i too know every man as a smaller muscle
i too when given the choice to bite and live
or sit and stay
will always remind the lesser
of my teeth.

when i was 8 i left the grate off the burn barrel
and watched 200 acres turn to flames
i ran to the old farmer's house. he already knew.
listen to me now, it's okay. you just wait and see
how green how green this is going to be.
recently i watched my life go up in these flames
char black too and thought *my god what if it's true?*
but i swear to you as far as i can see
she's coming back

        green.   green.   green.

i want to make love to me
the way only i can make love to me

i want to sit by myself at the bar
buy her a whiskey and cheers
to the lucky bastard that i am

i want to hold her back from running
into our house on fire
make her watch something burn
without her inside of it

i want to bloody her boss's nose
at the holiday party
sleep outside her door
get on my fucking knees
cry big man tears
tell her the truth
that i stalk her ig stories
with a fake account with my name backwards

i want to break into her phone
while she's sleeping
turn on the light
yell *what's this? what the fuck is this?!*

divorce her
then push her into the bathroom
at our son's birthday party
kiss her with all of my regret

i want legs around me that run into the ocean
high tide like only i run into the ocean high tide

and then i want to go as deep
as i can inside of her
finally meet her sound with sound
give her fists and fists full of sand
the pulse of her arteries tied off

then circle my hands around her wrists
pull them above her head
and finally know
what it fucking means
to tie
the hands of
god

when i was 6 i fell on a broken window
once i realized no one was coming
i stopped screaming
and pulled the shard from my middle.
this is life for some of us.
this has been life for me.

it's all magic. we just explain it away.
an african gray parrot lives seventy-five years
and tells stories.
in english.

a 12-year-old girl with stage four melanoma cancer
has three months to live
a small town prays
she lives.
she's me.

phytoplankton are the pastures of the seas
they look like tiny gorillas
produce half of the oxygen in the atmosphere
more than our forests and jungles combined
their carbon alone single-handedly combats climate change

only the holy book surveys the fire
the safe is melted into the earth

two pink dolphins in the amazon
use echolocation to find food beneath a river bed
share an anaconda lunch

my grandmother the sunday school teacher
leaves my grandfather at 65 years old
falls in love with the town drunk
and is loved for the first time in her life
and then dies young.
and then dies loved.

there is an island of sea dragons
thousands of submarine iguanas dive into the sea to eat
thirty min. one breath. all they have
or their muscles will seize up in the ice water
today all of them climb out. full-bellied.

thank you love!
the umbilical cord was wrapped three times
triple nuchal. not four. my baby boy enters the world
screaming pink.

if the polar ice caps melt
the current stagnates
life no longer exists

thank you love!
for the ice
hard as it is
hard as it is

there is a whale called the eden whale
fifteen tons and adapted to the low oxygen due to pollution
to survive she swims to the surface
opens her mouth and waits
and the fish
they jump right in.

you've forgotten that where you go when you dream
may be where you are actually awake.

you don't need graph paper
a couch in some city office
you need to remember your awe

who's to say
you need only
to swim up to the light
open your mouth wide?
who's to say?
who's to say love?
that it all won't jump right in.

i want to be in a 90's country music video with you

i want it rainin' and not stoppin' anytime soon
i want a thousand miles from nowhere
a screen door flappin' in the wind
i want your first time
i want july lightning
i want the roar on the hood of that ford

i want you riding a wild horse
me writing you to never come home from cheyenne
i want to be waitressing in amarillo when i see you again
lookin' better than you've ever looked
damn your painted-on wranglers!
damn your steel-toed boots and lariat hat
why'd. you. come. in. here. lookin'. like. that.

flashback to rope swing over your mama's pond
flashback to you leaving for the army
flashback to you drunk and yelling
and me kickin' you out with your dog
flashback to years later your wedding day
me standing in the back of the church
flashback to you seeing me
and never saying your vows

there's a '78 chevy parked outside still runnin'
git in honey
put your hand on my thigh
tear off the rearview mirror
the music has ended now
and there's nothin' but miles of dust
nothin' but miles of dust
left of us

i admit it
my no contact is bullshit.
as if god is not love and in everything we touch
as if i tell god i'm not available for your random i miss you text!
god damn it god!
i'm trying to convince us all i am over you
and the sun in your mouth
and tattooed sleeve
your laugh that heals the coral reef

god i must stop stalking you from a fake account.

no.
i must die on this hill.
holistic psychologist and integrity and swords and motherhood
and horses too young to impale!!

fuck the war i miss you.

and we are ants and the universe is being sucked into a black hole
everytime we dream and
it's. all. so. fucking. stupid.
ask the cancer kid.
ask me at 12 in nebraska medical center cancer wing
i would have said can't you see how much you hurt me?
and
i've thought of you every single waking
and closed-eye hour
and
i'm in greece alone
dancing with a man that doesn't smell like you
and
i still love you.

and we're all worm shit!
and sloughed off cells that gather as dust in window sills
i want two weeks locked in a cabin in the alps with you.
i want you to make a photography book of our hands.

you read mary oliver and i cover myself in hot oil and light the match

you say i am your home
i curl into the pea inside a thousand stacked mattresses
your mouth
your hot spit
all the bodies before embalming
that were buried alive
and scratched out the lining of their coffins.

i've lost fifteen pounds since you
i should fuck eight spartans immediately.
(you run in the veins of every leaf)

my heart is the monster on the twilight zone
eating the wing of the plane that only i can see.
my heart is chris cornell walking out the last time with his acoustic
it's been seven hours and sixteen days.
my heart a muscled ball of blood that is not going to beat forever!
a muscled ball of blood that's not going to beat forever
that hears you say my name on a podcast
the way only you say my name
and goes awol.
a soldier turning from the smoke
remembering finally
this is not my war.

i knew as soon as i got on the call
that i would not be doing ayahuasca
in joshua tree with peter pan.

fuck.
i am wendy.
the children and the blue nightdress and
and i've already been to neverland!
i can not follow the lost boy out the window
or sew shadows to hairless dicks

i loved him. he called me star.
and then cut stars for the mermaids
we were only trying to drown her they say

day 1
he's in neverland
my body is titanium.
no pixie could lift
everything becomes loud when i put it down

day 2
i think of nothing but heart cells in a petri dish
how within seconds two beat as one
birthmark under his eye
the window stays open and
i shake in my sleep

day 3
i clean twelve trash bags from my home.
the hardened paintbrushes. the night in sedona
you climbed in the bathtub with me.
then the hope went in
the horrible hope

wendy's tears on the third day sound like clay breaking
i do it under two layers of down
the wings i wrap around the other way
i don't wake the children

day 4
i say thank you to pineal gland
and swollen lids
and tarot cards of knights and swords
and hannah who came and held me
the kids are hungry
i break the yoke
i teach them helping verbs

day 5
my daughter gives me a crocheted rag
for my tea so i don't burn my hand
peter
wendy knows love
and it doesn't fly from the window

day 6
i throw away birth control
i feel every sharp edge man-made hormones
have numbed for fifteen years
i turn the wheel in my sternum that took the shape of you
until it unscrews and goes in the bag too
i whisper through the ether that i miss you.
i miss you. i miss you.

day 7
i make closet space
i close the window. it's warmer now.
i wonder if you hear it lock from there.
i pick up my pen again
and i write one thing only

every god
that has forgotten how to weep
i will call a boy.

when he was fucking our neighbor
with a kitchen sign that said wine time!
i flew to LA rented a piece of shit car
and took the first exit
where a demon could sit comfortably
order a meat sandwich
dip it in au jus
lick his fingers
and no one would question it

pasadena. a scorpion spray painted on the window
a speaker with a bass that was hissing
it was noon.
a fucking tuesday.
satan himself at the bar
god i was wearing a swimsuit cover up
heels strapped up my leg
a black swan
rummaged through a whorehouse shared closet
i pointed at his tattoo
prison he said the third time
from three layers of voice
one was a scream i needed to siphon
like an end scene
from a faceless shroud
he bought my tequila in crinkled bills
a rotting that made me pulse
i fisted his greasy hair leaned into him and said
something no poem should repeat
he made one stop in his low rider.
a strip mall cvs.
came out with bottles of cheap red
and bars of 99% chocolate
dry and bitter as hell
he was a cactus in my mouth
the motel was $46 a night
we paid for two.
didn't talk.
we slept a few hours at a time
on a mattress stripped bare

i looked like someone he had hit
he was more muscle than i had swallowed
whose pussy is this?
whose pussy is this?!
i cried once.
hour fifty-two or so he reached it
and held it for a moment
and he fucked it
on its side
stomach and bent up
against the tv stand and off the end
my head on the floor
once i thought he was going to pull a handful of hair
from my scalp.
this was the first and only time
i've slapped a grown man across the face
blacked an eye
this image of him
pouring sweat from his black curls
into my mouth
saying something in spanish
at some point i had a dream
i had checked into a place i would never leave
early and seventy-two hours later i left squinting
sun a forgotten torture
the weakness you feel in your elbows and
tell your legs to walk.
i blocked his contact.
i got off the plane.

you are forgiven
i kissed his cheek.
made dinner for the kids.
the carrara was polished.
he had cut peonies and put them in a cup of water
i took one in my fist
so light pink it was almost white
her entire head laying there open
and squeezed
until an oil
dripped
down
my arm

how you tear at your wings
but some men are just cocoons
(growing rooms. empty tombs.)
and i don't care what they say
women like us aren't meant to stay

year three of medical school
i learned the name of every capillary
which is to say
i know the name of the thinnest rivers of me
that you swam
femoral
iliac
carpal arches
mountains of ojai
christmas eve yellow fondue pot
the cold creek i bathed

but rivers dry
capillaries die
when they do
you lose what
they touched
the appendage turns back
biting nerve and the burn
numbs and weeks later
becomes the limb you drag

asking you to not reach for me
to step out. to dry and not look back
was not me loving myself more than i loved you
it was the scalpel in my hand
my eyes winced closed
to my own limb

he didn't know my name our first morning
he'd tell that story at every party
pissed me off.
he was never the man that opens doors
and every flower he gave me had veiny white roots
still wet from the ground and he held them
like he held my chin leaning in. he breathed me.
when i met his mother i was high. in heavy air.
and didn't take my hand out of his back pocket
and driving home he said *she hates you*
and i said *good. fuckin' good.*
and he almost flipped his truck kissing me
and we never did anything right
but fuck and fight
like the night the coyote killed our little dog
i screamed i hated him and he screamed
we could never have a kid
who would call the school when it was sick? we can't remember shit!
and he was right.
all our love did was fall and fall and keep falling
and forgot to reach for rocks. condoms.
or buckets for under all the leaks
forgot to shower alone.
forgot to whisper.
forgot to end.

remember the midsummer night
we chased marine layer to wood?
we had wings made of thinnest silk
slept on moss
we were supposed to be cold
i thought it would be cold

sometimes you are in the painted piano
the one with broken keys
that sits in the rain in manhattan
that people leave pennies on

the whistling child selling flowers
at the intersection of reseda and ventura

the medicine eyes of a stray
that walked up to my porch
one sunday morning

it's 1964 your hair is slicked
we're sharing a cigarette about to kill
a man you say must die
you nod
i put it out under my boot

we homestead. the children get chickenpox
we let them itch and scar.

some cult. our heads are shaved
i've been eating dandelion weed for two weeks.
you make me bitter tea
order me not to masturbate or
unsheathe my sword
i keep sneaking into your yurt
you don't ask me to leave

you are when the plane drops
and i know again how deep my middle goes

i'm barely 16 trembling in the back of your pickup
i whisper i won't fall unless you ask me to
you ask me to.

you are the end of the mayan calendar
there's no time to cry
we are dancing to jackie wants a black eye
the world flashes white
we hold on to the very end.

i have a woman talk to my inner child
to figure out why the hell i broke up
with fifty men in four years

and wouldn't you know
my inner child is
still madly in love with
charles ingalls.

sideways grin
coal on his face
dimples deep as the mississippi

charles who built our little house on the prairie
and pawned his fiddle to buy me a ring
charles convincin' mr edwards to take the orphans
charles rehabilitatin' the alcoholic
charles racin' against time
to stop the runaway caboose

charles put down laura's horse!
he's sufferin' charles
she's gonna cry for days
but you had to do it charles
you had to

charles
build me bookshelves
i'm openin' up a school
charles the baby is cold
pluck another chicken for the featherbed!

charles you just wait
you're gonna love me
you're gonna taste a country you've been thirstin' for
i can milk a jersey
i can fight the pack of coyotes off the dog
i can keep you so warm
you don't even know you need poems left for you on the breakfast table
but you need poems left for you on the breakfast table

charles come home
it's almost winter
charles let me kiss off the day
charles put your hand over my mouth
the babies will hear

charles listen.
no more hippies in range rovers
no more tech bros in teslas

i want you charles ingalls
right off your quarter horse
and stinkin' brown
in your suspenders
by the fire you built us
your fiddle across your lap
callin' me some name you made up for me
like goldie. or boss. or blue.
that nobody's callin' me but you

i want you charles ingalls
to be here already!
your leathered hands
hikin' up my cotton dress
sayin' real quiet
come here
come here
where you been
i missed you

i forgive you
for the lies so you could stay
for pointing at truth
and asking her to wear better clothes
i forgive you for longing for a man
to keep you dry
when it's you wringing the sky

i forgive you
for your parenting during the divorce
your daughter slipping a post it under your door
mommy are you sad?
i forgive you for answering no.

i forgive you for the pity kisses
i forgive you for trying to heal
his depression
with your naked body.

i forgive you for marrying at 20
for kissing the bartender in san francisco
i forgive you that you've been alone so long
that together feels like being buried in sand
a something you can't stand out of.

i forgive you standing at the arno in florence
and planning how to fake your death
i forgive you for giving away your dog lady
when the babies were born
i forgive you for slamming your little brothers fingers in the door
that game of hide and seek

for the texts you sent to your mother
asking her to love you

i forgive you for the first weekend your ex took the kids
when you called begging wildly to bring them back
screaming at the top of your lungs

and i forgive you finally for all the times
you were handed the rarest pearl in the world
and remembered all of this
and handed it back
instead of standing at the table
dissolving it in a glass of wine
and
raising it high
before
you drank it down.

an elegy.
goodbye waxing my asshole.
goodbye holding my pee.
goodbye hugging old white men
ob   li   ga   tor   y
goodbye distracting political noise
goodbye wearing flats for short boys
goodbye sin
goodbye forgetting i'm a ten.
(ever ever ever again)
goodbye pisces with the large d
goodbye libra squared too afraid to dive
goodbye ten thousand spoons
(when all i need is a knife)
goodbye broken can opener.
and scorpio times three.
goodbye pretending two o's
could satisfy me
goodbye men that don't read
or keep plants alive
(what a bore)
goodbye men that love e.d.m.
goodbye pretending *i don't require more*
goodbye cnn.
goodbye socks with holes.
goodbye helping boys find their souls
goodbye hangovers. slimy tofu.
goodbye everything white jesus loves you
goodbye LA bullshit
your vibe is so low!
goodbye to the heels blistering my toe
goodbye to the *i don't understand poetry* bro.
goodbye thick white sunscreen. goodbye bras.
goodbye flaneur! goodbye plastic straws!
goodbye lover boy
and the *separating sad guy*
still lives with his wife
goodbye to everyone who doesn't see
the *miracle of this life*

goodbye thin kissing lips
goodbye long-distance relationships
goodbye men that don't bring their plate to the sink
goodbye politics and illusion and partisan think
goodbye red-nailed texans that wear coats of mink
goodbye all my exes
waste of ink!
goodbye mushy fries!
goodbye un-touching thighs!
goodbye inaudible sighs!
goodbye pretending i'm less of a mother.
less of a lover.
less of a warrior god.
goodbye scrubbing the canvas of my life
goodbye to anyone and everyone
who forgets
i am divine light
goodbye!
goodbye!
goodbye!

thank you

Lilly, Jack, and Clara.
(sun. moon. and stars.)

Aunt Lisa- teaching me how to love. for the way you are looking at me in my
baby photos. for never ever ever letting me go.

Women in Poems and Power- thank you for loving you.
thank you for loving me.

Dad- teaching me how to be brave, how to work. for jumping in the concrete
bowl, stirring it yourself when the truck broke down. for the acid
eating your hands and through your shoes. teaching me if you keep moving,
you won't harden. thank you.

Mom- i love you.

Heartbreak- you fine tuner. you good good death. you expander.
you poem maker. thank you.

Cooper- for all of the tech help, the hundreds of hours.

Mama God- for breath. the color in my arm.
so so grateful you let me stay here.
for the poetry. thank you.